Vietnam
COMBAT FROM
THE COCKPIT

Robert F. Dorr

Airlife
England

For Don Kilgus

Airlife Publishing Ltd.

7 St. John's Hill, Shrewsbury, England

On the front cover: *Upon completion of its 100th combat mission, Caroline, F-4D Phantom 66-7767 (FG) of the 433rd Tactical Fighter Squadron, 8th Tactical Fighter Wing, Ubon, Thailand, trails red smoke to celebrate.* Steve Mosier

Inset on the front cover: *It has become almost cliche to point out that every time valor was tested on the battlefield, Americans prevailed. Major Joe Viviano (center) of the 20th Special Operations Squadron, or Green Hornets, located at Nha Trang, South Vietnam, joins crew members of his UH-1F Huey in holding up a captured North Vietnamese flag.* Joe Viviano

On the back cover: *Painted in the markings of North Vietnam's infamous air ace Colonel Tomb, the US Air Force Museum's MiG-17 prepares to join a Vietnam-era exhibit in June 1988. Only the second MiG-17 to be placed on display in the United States, this aircraft shows the restoration skills of history-conscious workers at the Dayton, Ohio, museum.* David W. Menard

On the frontispiece: *Boring toward North Vietnam at the height of Rolling Thunder combat operations in the 1967-68 period, Captain Steve Mosier of the 433rd Tactical Fighter Squadron wears a view of an F-4D Phantom in the reflection of his flight goggles. Helmet and goggles in use during the Southeast Asia conflict were much bulkier than those employed today.* Steve Mosier

On the title page: *Into the sunset. F-105 Thunderchief and KC-135 Stratotanker during flight refueling operations with a setting sun behind them.* Donald W. Kilgus

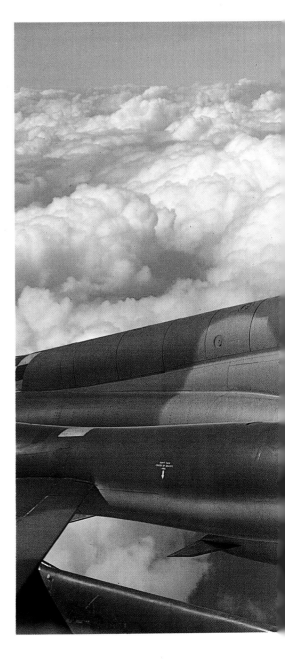

On the contents page: *High over the battle zone in December 1970, white-helmeted South Vietnamese pilot stares from his Northrop F-5A Freedom Fighter and presses toward the target. F-5A was one of the newer jet aircraft used successfully in the conflict and became the backbone of Saigon's air arm.* Cort Durocher

Contents

Acknowledgments	*6*	**Fighters**	*60*
A is for attack	*9*	**Who *are* those guys?**	*84*
Big jet, little jet	*27*	**The MiG killers**	*105*
Southeast Asia sharkmouths	*41*	**Survivors**	*118*

Acknowledgments

This book is dedicated to Donald W. Kilgus, who helped in its preparation and who went over to Southeast Asia every year we were in the war. On the green slope at Arlington where we lay our heroes to rest, there is a space that belongs to Don—all honor to his name.

While mistakes are the fault of the author, this book would not have been possible without the assistance of the pilots and other veterans quoted on these pages, and the photographers whose work appears here. Their names appear in the text.

The material on the RC-135M Combat Apple aircraft is quoted with permission from *SAC Tanker Operations in the Southeast Asia War,* by Charles K. Hopkins, published in 1979 by the Office of the Historian, Headquarters, Strategic Air Command. The quote from Major Philip Combies is used with permission from *Aces and Aerial Victories: The United States Air Force in Southeast Asia, 1965-1973,* published in 1976 by the Office of Air Force History, Headquarters USAF.

I particularly want to thank Larry Davis; Joseph G. Handelman; Bill Henry; Martin Judge; Kay Kilgus; Donald S. McGarry; David W. Menard; Peter B. Mersky; R. J. Mills, Jr.; Tim Parker; Eric Renth; and Stephen R. Stephen.

This book is intended to take the reader into the air war in Vietnam through the medium of top-quality, previously unpublished photographs. The original plan was to include every aircraft type used by the Air Force, Navy and Marine Corps in the Southeast Asia conflict (Army aviation, its advocates acknowledge, is a separate subject). All of the principal aircraft types *are* included here. The few aircraft types that were left out have not been forgotten. That, of course, is the central message of this volume: We should never forget.

Robert F. Dorr

Its war finished, this Marine Corps CH-46F Sea Knight helicopter 156459 (side number ET-2) belonging to squadron HMH-262 basks in the unusual sunshine at Kaneohe Bay, Hawaii, on 16 January 1975, only months before the evacuation of Saigon. Helicopters transformed the war in Southeast Asia, and the Sea Knight is representative of all of the thousands that did the job over the long years of the war.
Joseph G. Handelman

A is for attack

Commander Jim McBride

One gray morning we rolled in and smeared napalm across a mob of very angry NVA who were attacking a Special Forces camp up near Pleiku. It was one of those rare moments when everything clicked. We were cleared in to the target. We had good communication. The voice of the Army officer on the ground was crystal clear. "They're coming through the wire, they're coming through the wire!"

I snapped the airplane out of the roll and had a solid swath of NVA uniforms spread out in front of me. This is unusual in daylight, even the murky daylight in the mist that hangs over most of Southeast Asia, but I could actually *see* the *muzzle flashes* where they were shooting at our guys. We went on in, delivered our ordnance pretty accurately, and had the satisfaction of knowing that we'd halted an attack that would have killed many of our fellow Americans.

I've been asked again and again, why did I choose to become an attack pilot? After all, Tom Cruise never made a movie called Top Bomb. Mud movers, they call us. Whether we're flying deep interdiction strikes behind enemy lines—going as far as Hanoi at times—or supporting our troops on the battlefield, the job is pretty devoid of any glamor or glory.

I guess the truth is, carrying bombs and fighting down in the weeds is a very special challenge. The naval aviator on a pitching carrier deck, the Marine pilot at an expeditionary airfield, the Air Force flier at his own airstrip—*all* attack pilots face a challenge. The attack guy has to get down low in bad weather and defeat everything the enemy can throw at him, whether it's guns, missiles or MiGs. The air-to-air fighter jocks get more attention, but it's us attack guys who win the wars.

Captain Hubert G. King

For me, coming out of jets, the Douglas A-1 Skyraider was quite a shock. It looked ugly at first but after you flew it a while it began to look beautiful. It had incredible performance and was the most satisfying airplane I've ever flown.

The Skyraider, it was named. We called it the Spad, evoking images of the romantic past of aviation. Unlike those Fast Movers in jets we often flew with the wind in our faces. And the Spad could carry anything in the Bomb Dump, and put it right on top of the target.

It could carry an infinite mix of weapons tailored for any target. It was built like a brick pagoda. It would bring you back, full of holes, with tree trunks imbedded in the wings or parts of *people,* even, but it would bring you back.

The only thing it wouldn't do was fly fast in level flight. But in a dive the acceleration was amazing.

It was unforgiving only on the ground. In flight, you really had to horse it around if you wanted to get in trouble by over-controlling but once you learned to tap-dance on the rudder pedals it was no problem.

It was old. It was cantankerous. Some called it a relic. The Spad dripped oil, coughed smoke, demanded a deft touch on the rudder, and was never easy to fly. But this airplane had the staying power to remain over a battle zone for extended periods, the ordnance capacity to carry almost endless bombs and rockets, and the sturdiness to take punishment from ground fire and survive.

An Air Force veteran

On 30 April 1975, as the end closed in, as North Vietnamese tanks crashed through the city outskirts and headed for the President's residence in Saigon, evacuating Americans looked up as a lone A-1H Skyraider churned through the light smoke and overcast. Flown by an intrepid South Vietnamese, the Skyraider flicked its wings in defiance, behaved as if the war was not over, and laid down harassing fire at the victors from Hanoi who spread through the city.

In September 1960, with approval of President Eisenhower, US Navy Lieutenant Ken Moranville went to Bien Hoa to teach the Vietnamese to fly the AD-6 Skyraider. Fourteen years and eight months later, just after noon on that final day in April, the Vietnamese A-1H Skyraider was hit by a shoulder-mounted SAM

continued on page 12

Previous page
In April 1965, with few Americans aware of a build-up in Vietnam, an A-1E Skyraider 132615 (airplane 4) of the First Air Commando Squadron scythes along the coast near Saigon carrying a centerline fuel tank and cluster bomb units. Flown by a single Air Force pilot, this Skyraider was set up with a multi-place crew, hence the Blue Room under the aft canopy, now an empty space except during long ferry trips when Spad drivers returned to their home units with fine wine or ratan furniture. In an identical A-1E on 10 March 1966, Major Bernard F. Fisher landed in the midst of a battle at A Shau to rescue a fellow pilot while under intense fire and earn the first Medal of Honor awarded by the Air Force in Southeast Asia. Perrin Gower

On Yankee Station aboard USS Bon Homme Richard (CVA-31) in 1967, a wall of noise engulfs the crowded wooden deck of the carrier as the Barn Owls of attack squadron VA-215 prepare for a mission. A-1H Skyraider 139665 (side number NP-562) carries only two pods of 2.75 in. folding fin aircraft rockets (FFAR) recessed behind a disposable nose cone. Because operations on the flight deck could be thrown awry by a single false step, the movement of men and machines before a launch was an elaborate mix of discipline and choreography. Ron Lord

10

continued from page 9

missile and went down in flames, just as North Vietnam's troops raised their flag over Saigon. For Americans in Vietnam the Skyraider had been first in and last out.

Douglas chief designer Edward H. Heinemann

Perhaps the most unusual or interesting part of development of the A-4 was that when it was first submitted to the Navy there were several people in the Navy who made unkind remarks about my enthusiasm, my unrealistic approach, my irresponsibilities and so on. I also ran into considerable doubt among my own design team who had the 30,000 pound weight so ingrained in their thinking that they thought I was absolutely mad to try to do it for less than half. This resulted in my locking myself in my office one morning very early and before I went home that day I had an outline drawing of the airplane and a preliminary weight analysis with which I was satisfied. I called my design team together and gave them each a blueprint of my layout and said, "I think this can be done. It will take a tough SOB to do it and before you say it I

continued on page 14

Sundance *was a Cessna A-37B Dragonfly 69-6348 fresh off the factory line and assigned to the 604th Fighter Squadron at Bien Hoa. It looked small, but pilots were quick to point out that it weighed 14,000 pounds and could carry nearly its own weight in ordnance to attack the bad guys.* Cort Durocher

continued from page 12

will say it, I am he. I would like to have you all join my team. Anyone who doesn't wish to join, there is the door." No one left the room.

Commander Everett Alvarez, Jr.

You have to remember that the A-4 was designed by Heinemann at Douglas Aircraft for only *one reason,* and that was to carry the Mark 7 [nuclear] weapon. The Mark 7 was a big, round thing and this plane was built around it. When the Mark 7 was hoisted up on the centerline rack you had only inches to spare. By the time we were flying [in 1963], we had graduated to the Mark 28 which was a much smaller [nuclear] weapon and this A-4 Skyhawk, with its stork-like legs designed for that big bomb, was suddenly useful for a lot of conventional bombing tasks.

Major Dorsie Paige, USMC

I'm flying a fast FAC road recce mission over Laos in a two-seat TA-4F with an observer in the back seat. We run into some pretty pesky ground fire. I throw the Skyhawk into a tight turn above the North Vietnamese gunners and am immediately grateful that Ed Heinemann designed the Scooter to be small and maneuverable. They say the cockpit of a Skyhawk is so narrow you can't completely unfold a map in it. And the skin of the airplane is so thin you can puncture it with a fountain pen. But they made the "bantam bomber" nimble enough to get out of harm's way—at least most of the time.

A rifle bullet goes through the side of the fuselage below my head, goes in a perpendicular line so that it goes through *both* of my legs, and passes out the other side of the plane. I am suddenly bleeding all over the place with a bullet wound becoming extremely painful. We finish our FAC [forward air controller] job and by some miracle I'm able to bring the plane back through night and fog to a safe landing at Chu Lai. My hat's off to the designer of the A-4 Skyhawk, one tough airplane.

Lieutenant Commander Tom Patterson, bombardier-navigator

When some of the critics first took a look at the A-6 Intruder they said, hey, this isn't right, the *pointed* end of the aircraft is supposed to be at the *front.* There was also some badmouthing when the Sunday Punchers of attack squadron VA-75 went over to 'Nam on the first combat cruise because the electronics on the A-6 had not yet been perfected at that time and was not working right much of the time. But when it *did* work right, the A-6 with its two-man crew—pilot and bombardier-navigator [BN]—could put a bomb on a dime, with pinpoint accuracy, at night and in bad weather. For years, the Air Force was embarrassed because it didn't have a bad-weather bomber to match the A-6.

In squadron VA-115, known as the Arabs and operating from the carrier *Constellation* (CVA-64), we had some very colorful Intruder attack planes, as well as the KA-6D tanker which was very similar. The tankers often had a stripe painted around the rear fuselage to distinguish them, and when the flight refueling "drogue" was extended the difference was quite obvious. Plus the fact that the KA-6D usually carried external fuel tanks while the A-6A and A-6E Intruders carried bombs.

Lt. Comdr. Art Merz leans forward in cockpit to check switches of A-4C Skyhawk 148454 whilst preparing to launch into combat from USS Shangri-La (CVS-38). Green-jacketed catapult crewmen affix the bridle which will send the Skyhawk into the air with its load of Mark 83 1,000 lb bombs. Deck crew sometimes uses chalk to record needed items of information inside the nose wheel well door. Merz' squadron, VA-12, was known as the Flying Ubangis until a Pentagon bigwig feared a racial connotation and ordered the change to Clinchers, but the skeleton Kiss of Death insignia remained the same even after the squadron later shifted to A-7 Corsairs. Jim McBride

On another 1970 mission in a different airplane, an A-4C Skyhawk which is probably airplane 147782 (side number AJ-411), Merz displays the Kiss of Death marking while turning to approach the carrier. Refueling probe, radio antenna, navigation light and under-wing fuel tanks are all visible. Jim McBride

North American RA-5C Vigilante 156608 (side number NE-610) of Heavy Attack Squadron Seven, or RVAH-7, flying off the West Coast prior to deployment to Southeast Asia. US Navy

Final version of the Skyhawk, the A-4M, did not reach the combat zone but had internal improvements based on Vietnam experience. Wearing very different VMAT-102 markings from those in previous photo, A-4M Skyhawk 159491 (side number SC-2) shows its brilliant colors at MCAS Yuma, Arizona, in May 1976. Douglas Barbier

19

Grumman KA-6D Intruder tanker 152921 (side number NF-520) of the Arabs of VA-115 flying during a period of shore duty at NAF Atsugi, Japan, on 20 January 1978. The US Navy's gray and white color scheme was complemented by bright-colored markings during the Vietnam era and until the late 1970s. Masumi Wada

A-6E Intruder 152895 (side number AG-504) of the Tigers of VA-65 at NAS Oceana, Virginia, on 20 October 1977. Protruding from the aircraft below the word NAVY is the equipment bay which crews call the birdcage. When this gear package is extended, a maintenance man can sit and work inside the rear fuselage. Robert F. Dorr

*Vought A-7E Corsair 158827 (side
number AA-400) of the Sunliners
of VA-81 practicing aboard USS
Forrestal (CVA-59) on 2 August
1977.* Robert L. Burns

Tail of A-7E Corsair 156848 (side number NL-405) of the Shrikes of VA-93 operating from USS Kitty Hawk *(CVA-63) during a visit to Andrews AFB, Maryland, on 7 April 1979. During 1972 operations against North Vietnam, Shrikes under Commander David Moss inflicted a heavy toll on the enemy.* Robert F. Dorr

A-7E Corsair 156823 (side number NG-406) of the Argonauts of VA-147, assigned to USS Constellation (CVA-64) during a postwar stopover at Andrews AFB, Maryland, on 26 May 1979. Argonauts under Commander James Hill were the first squadron to introduce the A-7 to combat. Robert F. Dorr

Big jet, little jet

A B-57 Canberra pilot

The B-57 was a source of unending amazement for me. It was the US-built version of the British Canberra jet bomber, of course, and it was the last light bomber ever used by our air force. A B-57 could drop bombs on a Viet Cong position being defended by all sorts of guns, take punishment, and bring its crew home. One of our planes absorbed 227 bullet holes from a 7.62 mm or 12.7 mm gun, including some that ruptured a hydraulic line, and it still brought the crew back. I was hit by anti-aircraft fire near the Mekong Delta and was so badly shot up there was black smoke and pieces of metal blowing back into my slipstream, and I had a partial loss of the flight controls, but that B-57 got me all the way back to the airfield almost 100 miles away. Some of the holes were so large a ground crew guy could shove his fist into them.

We were among the first into the war, flying from Bien Hoa as

continued on page 28

Belonging to the Burlington, Vermont-based Green Mountain Boys, or 134th Defense Systems Evaluation Squadron, was up-sized Vietnam veteran EB-57B Canberra 52-1503, seen at Andrews AFB, Maryland, on 21 May 1977. The EB-57B was used to simulate Soviet aircraft to test the readiness of US air defenses. Canberra was a nickname applied by the British and was not often used by Americans, but the US Air Force did adopt it officially. Robert F. Dorr

27

continued from page 27

early as 1964. Most people remember B-57s from that terrible 31 October 1964 Viet Cong mortar attack on Bien Hoa when five Canberra bombers were destroyed while parked in their hardstands. Or, worse, the 14 May 1965 incident when, without any help from the enemy, an accidental detonation set off a firestorm that blew *ten* Canberras to bits. But the fact is, the B-57 served with real distinction and its ability to take punishment from the enemy was only one of its strong attributes.

Colonel Preston Olinger

The first time I saw a B-52 up close, I thought, "What a huge behemoth of a device." The tip tank alone weighed 6,000 pounds. My crew chief told me the aircraft had enough electrical wiring inside to stretch out for five miles, like baling wire. He pointed at the thin metal skin of the fuselage and said that the B-52 had enough metal in it to make 5,000 garbage cans. And he pointed at the eight J57 engines and said that each of those was as powerful as a railroad locomotive. "And you know, sir," he said with a grin, "that's exactly what this thing flies like. It flies like eight locomotives pulling ten

continued on page 30

Except that no one is in the flight cabin, 55-0083 might be plowing through the sky on another mission over North Vietnam. Markings on the fuselage to represent bomb missions in the Hanoi region are all accurate, including the red silhouette of a MiG-21 fighter shot down by this bomber's fire control operator (tail gunner), A1C Albert E. Moore. Robert F. Dorr

28

continued from page 28
thousand garbage cans wrapped in
five miles of baling wire."

We began Arc Light
operations in South Vietnam in
early 1965. We also brought the
war to an end during December
1972 when, for eleven days, we
used the B-52 to pound targets
around Hanoi—and forced the
North Vietnamese into a
settlement. In those eleven days,
we lost *eighteen* B-52s in combat,
after going through the seven
previous years without a loss. We
also shot down two MiG-21s,
dropped thousands of tons of
conventional bombs, and brought
about the 27 January 1973 cease-

fire agreement which ended
American participation in Vietnam.

A Strategic Air Command historian

Typical reconnaissance and
support missions in [Southeast
Asia] were called Box Top, Cotton
Candy, and Iron Lung. From the
latter part of 1967 onwards, the
principal reconnaissance mission
flown by tanker aircraft was
Combat Apple. Normally, RC-135Ms
flew Combat Apple missions, but
occasionally an RC-135C or RC-
135D would have to augment the
force. Combat Apple involved
flying 12-hour orbits over the Gulf
continued on page 32

*South Vietnamese pilot and crew
chief stand in front of F-5B
Freedom Fighter 65-10586 at Bien
Hoa airbase near Saigon in
December 1970. The two-seat F-5B
was a dwarf compared to the F-4
Phantom, but it proved highly
effective for bombing and strafing
lightly defended targets inside
South Vietnam.* Cort Durocher

Big guy or little guy, the back seat of an F-4 Phantom can be cramped at times and lonely during those times when you're not cranking your head every which way to look for MiGs. Though it was one of the largest of fighters, the Phantom could feel small inside. The confines in the rear of F-4D Phantom 66-7549, including the rearview mirrors, had changed very little between the Vietnam conflict and 18 May 1988, when I took this self-portrait. Robert F. Dorr

continued from page 30

of Tonkin, and later over Laos too, collecting electronic intelligence with special attention to picking up indications of Fan Song radar signals. These signals were indications of the existence of SAMs [surface-to-air missiles]. Areas of intense search for them included North Vietnam, Hainan Island and the Demilitarized Zone. At first there were about 50 or 60 Combat Apple missions a month, but they soon leveled off to about 30. The Combat Apple aircraft regularly flew other SAC [Strategic Air Command] reconnaissance missions as well. This had replaced an earlier mission which was also the collection of electronic intelligence. In this case it involved peripheral reconnaissance over the Yellow Sea, East China Sea and Gulf of Tonkin with the objective of collecting electronic intelligence on the enemy order of battle.

When the RC-135M went "up north," the MiGs came out. For a time Hanoi's authorities toyed with the idea of intercepting an RC-135M. F-4 Phantoms accompanied the Combat Apple aircraft on its trip to the edge of enemy terrain, the Phantoms remaining so close

that their own radar images blurred with those of the RC-135M. Unaware that the RC-135M was escorted by "little friends," the MiGs came after what they thought was a big slow Boeing only to find accompanying F-4s looking down their throats. After this happened a few times, an unspoken truce took effect.

An RC-135 reconnaissance airplane's navigator

The MiGs used to come up, start toward us, and change their minds. We were flying offshore. Unarmed. Supposedly unafraid. And we knew damn well that, one day, the MiGs weren't going to turn around and go home while our big silvery bird stood out over the coast and made a beautiful target for them. We were not only unarmed, we were meat on the table for those MiGs.

Fortunately, the one time they did come out and try to jump us, we had some "little friends" in the neighborhood. A pair of US Navy F-8 Crusaders from a carrier in the Gulf were snuggled under our wing, where they wouldn't present a radar image to the bad guys.

Barely a speck in a brilliant Southeast Asia sky, Cessna A-37B Dragonfly of the US Air Force's 604th Fighter Squadron returns from a combat mission in September 1970. The A-37B was one of the smallest combat aircraft but was used effectively by both American and South Vietnamese units. Cort Durocher

In Southeast Asia, TA-4F two-seat Scooters flew FAC (forward air) control) and artillery spotting missions. In the post-Vietnam era, Skyhawks were employed for training, especially air combat maneuver (ACM) training where they acted as aggressors and simulated the role of MiG-17s in attacking friendly fighters. Simulating a Third World MiG, replete with blotches that look like bullet holes, TA-4F Skyhawk 154331 (side number SC-31) of Yuma, Arizona-based Marine squadron VMAT-102 pauses during a visit to Andrews AFB, Maryland, 15 March 1980. Eugene L. Zorn

Also a Green Mountain aircraft, Martin B-57C Canberra 53-3856 of the 134th Defense Systems Evaluation Squadron, Vermont Air National Guard, was being employed to simulate Soviet aircraft when it visited Andrews AFB, Maryland, on 11 May 1979. The black paint scheme, however, is actually more typical of the pre-Vietnam Canberra. Robert F. Dorr

"Little friend" and much-loved carrier-based fighter, the Vought F-8 Crusader shot down twenty MiGs over Hanoi and flew thousands of successful air-to-air missions. F-8J Crusader 150680 (side number NP-107) of squadron VF-211 sits ashore following a cruise aboard USS Hancock (CVA-19). The date is 21 June 1974 and the fall of Saigon is still a year away. Bergagnini via Mills

Never before, never since, has any warplane quite captured the imagination like the Boeing B-52 Stratofortress, seen here in a postwar incarnation landing with braking chute. B-52s pulverized Hanoi in December 1972 bombing raids, but even then crews considered them "old." Yet today they remain in service in both conventional and nuclear bombing roles. Jim Benson

Probably the largest aircraft ever painted with shark teeth was EC-130E Hercules 62-1825, callsign CRICKET, of the 7th Airborne Command and Control Squadron, 388th Tactical Fighter Wing, at Korat AB, Thailand, in July 1973. This airborne command post wore the controversial dentures only for a very brief period. Donald L. Jay

Southeast Asia sharkmouths

Colonel Edward Hillding

I don't think there was another war in which the Brass Hats struggled so hard—or so unsuccessfully—to keep us from painting individual markings on our airplanes. There's a spirit among people who sit in cockpits and go into battle and the Brass doesn't always recognize that spirit. One of my captains with the unlikely name of Stephen R. Stephen came up with a *fantastic* design for sharks' teeth on the noses of our F-4E Phantoms, and a *four-star general* almost immediately told us they had to come off. We removed the distinctive markings from a couple of our airplanes but we kept thinking up reasons to delay, delay, delay. By the time it was noticed that we *still* had the offending sharks' teeth on the airplanes, we were caught up in the middle of very heavy fighting and there were other things to worry about.

Later on, the commander of the 388th Tactical Fighter Wing at Korat relented to the extent of decreeing that sharks' teeth were okay, but *only* on the F-4E Phantoms of the 469th squadron, and later the 34th squadron. The skipper's edict didn't prevent the Airborne Command Post weenies from painting teeth on their C-130 Hercules, or the F-105 jocks from devising some very creative snaggletooth emblems, or the EB-66 crews from adopting sharkmouth markings. A few of these examples of creativity actually survived for extended periods of time, but just as often some stuffed shirt from Headquarters would come along and spoil things for everybody. We never gave up, though, and we never lost that spirit.

An EB-66 electronic warfare officer (EWO)

It was supposed to be a bomber, based on the Navy's A-3 Skywarrior, but in fact it was always intended as a reconnaissance aircraft. We used it to jam the radar signals from Hanoi's surface-to-air missile network. You could send one EB-66 up there, right into the middle of it all, and the "sparks" we put out would throw their whole air defense system into total confusion. It was costly, of course, and we lost about half a dozen EB-66s in combat, but we were very, *very* effective.

A US Navy maintenance man

We always had a special feeling for the Sundowners of VF-111, the Navy fighter squadron that operated F-4B Phantoms from my carrier. The F-4 Phantom was the biggest, fastest, most expensive, most exciting airplane in the world and even if it wasn't perfect—its engines gave off a telltale cloud of smoke that told the enemy it was coming—it was one heck of a flying machine.

The Sundowners have been painting little teeth on the noses of their fighter planes for years. In the Southeast Asia conflict, those teeth appeared first on the squadron's Crusaders and later on its Phantoms. Unlike the Air Force guys, we were never harassed about having our own distinctive markings and no one would have dreamed of asking us to take the teeth off. Those teeth were like a badge of honor.

A US Air Force intelligence officer

The MiG-19 fighter, also known as the Farmer, was not in North Vietnam's inventory until nearly the end of the war when a few of them started showing up. On 10 May 1972, a pair of MiG-19s shot down Major Bob Lodge who had gotten three MiGs himself and who might have become the first ace of the war had he not given his life that day. This was one of the few instances when the MiG-19 was successful against our fighters.

The Nineteen was a twin-engine fighter and was probably seen by the Russians as an "interim" aircraft, although it may have had the distinction of being the first operational fighter capable of supersonic speed in level flight—a claim we often bestow on our F-100. The Russians were not big on twin-engine fighters at that time and the MiG-19 was only produced in moderate numbers.

The term "Chinese copy" might apply to the Shenyang F-6 version of the MiG-19 which has

continued on page 42

continued from page 41

been successful and was exported to Pakistan as well as North Vietnam. The MiG-19 was powered by two 7,165 lb thrust Tumansky RD-9B turbojets with afterburners. It could carry three 30 mm cannon plus rockets so if it ever got you in its sights, you were in deep trouble.

At Korat, Thailand, on 28 March 1973, with US fighting in Vietnam just ended but combat continuing in Laos and Cambodia, an F-4E Phantom heads on out carrying bombs and shark teeth. This 34th Tactical Fighter Squadron Phantom is seen passing parked EC-121 Constellations. Dan Kuebler

*At Da Nang in 1972, battle-garbed
Captain Tom Hanton stands in
front of his sharkmouthed F-4E
Phantom before climbing into the
cockpit. A back-seat Weapon
Systems Officer, Hanton was shot
down in June 1972 and held
prisoner by the North Vietnamese
until the end of the conflict.*
Thomas J. Hanton

Douglas EB-66C Destroyer 54-0438 of the 42nd Tactical Electronic Warfare Squadron at Korat AB, Thailand, in August 1972. The shark teeth marking on the nose was extremely unusual and reflected the high spirits of EB-66 crews. Donald L. Jay

Next page
No fangs, but colorful anyway. Identical to the Shenyang F-6 (MiG-19) fighters flown by the North Vietnamese, this aircraft belongs to the Black Spider squadron of the Pakistan Air Force. In the hands of Hanoi's pilots, the MiG-19 entered the conflict in its late stages and had modest success against US fighters. Larry Davis

At Korat airbase, Thailand, in November 1972, the snaggletooth insignia of the F-105G Thunderchief of the 17th Wild Weasel Squadron was the most innovative paint scheme going. Two-seat F-105Gs located North Vietnamese missile sites and attacked them with help from F-4 Phantoms. Larry Davis

48

Whatever may be painted on the outside, the man inside the aircraft is the key to success. Major Donald W. Kilgus snapped this self-portrait at the controls of an F-105F Thunderchief of the 17th Wild Weasel Squadron, Korat AB, Thailand. Kilgus was shot down during the Son Tay raid in such an aircraft in November 1970. Warning notice taped on the pilot's oxygen mask tells him the system is due for reinspection on 10 April 1972. Donald W. Kilgus

Hey Jude, *alias F-4E Phantom 68-317 of the 421st Tactical Fighter Squadron, part of the 366th Tactical Fighter Wing, sits on the ramp at Da Nang in 1972. Aircraft is equipped with a Northrop-built TISEO (target identification system, electro-optical)—in effect, a long-range TV camera—found in cylindrical fairing at wing's leading edge.* Larry Davis

DANGER
RESCUE
OPPOSITE SIDE
JET
DANGER
INTAKE
205
3F083
PHANTOM
FIXERS
INC.
WT
EVT
U S NAVY
GAC6
261306

Just released from the military aircraft storage center in Arizona wearing the markings of the Sundowners of VF-111, this Phantom is reporting for duty with the Marine Reserve's Hell's Angels of VMFA-321. F-4N Phantom 152968 (side number NL-205, storage number 8F 083) is a former F-4B which fought in Vietnam and is seen at Andrews AFB, Maryland, on 9 June 1979. Robert F. Dorr

Previous page
Weasel in the night. Two-seat Republic F-105F Thunderchief returning from a combat mission in about 1970 is framed by a sensational Vietnamese sunset. Donald W. Kilgus

F-105, the immortal Thud, as seen from a wingman's cockpit. Donald W. Kilgus

The Vought A-7D ground-attack aircraft, called Corsair II by the Navy but never given a popular name by the Air Force, managed to sport a few molars of its own. At Korat in December 1973, A-7D 70-988 of the 3rd Tactical Fighter Squadron brandishes its open jaws. Donald L. Jay

Fighters

Colonel Donald W. Kilgus

Flying the F-100, better known as the Hun or the Super Sabre, I think the most impressive thing I ever saw was going down to the Mekong Delta. Rice paddies, fully flooded, early morning, high humidity. You dropped a 750 lb bomb that would hit in that rice paddy and the first thing you would see, in addition to the geyser of water coming up, would be a doughnut-shaped cloud of moisture condensation from the shock wave of the bomb going off. And then you'd sit and you'd watch and it looked like piranhas coming up to the surface—and that would be the shrapnel, falling in the water for as much as a mile to a mile and a half from the point of impact. And the first time you saw that, you'd say, "Oh, and we're dropping *that* close to *friendly* troops!" So you were very aware of the weapons' effects.

continued on page 62

In May 1963, Americans already were becoming embroiled in a conflict in the rain jungles of Southeast Asia, but F-100 Super Sabre pilots of the 416th Tactical Fighter Squadron (Silver Knights) stationed at Misawa AB, Japan, did not yet know it. F-100D Super Sabre 55-3740 wears the plain aluminum in which the Hun went to war a few months later, the buzz number (FW-740) which disappeared in the early days of the war, and a PACAF (Pacific Air Forces) badge on the tail which was dispensed with before the 416th TFS reached the combat zone.
Donald W. Kilgus

continued from page 60

We used the F-100 briefly for missions into North Vietnam, and on 4 April 1965, I got a "probable" kill of a MiG-17 by chasing him down into some coffee-brown smaze and popping off 20 mm bursts at him. I just came down on the trigger until I thought I was at about 6,500 feet and I was still firing when I pulled the G in. I literally scraped the belly of my F-100 against the Gulf of Tonkin pulling out and I didn't actually see the MiG go in, but to this day I'm absolutely confident that I got him.

But throughout the war, of course, the F-100 was our most important "mud mover"—the airplane we depended upon to carry the napalm, bombs and rockets to the Viet Cong. We fought the war down low, almost in the middle of our own infantrymen, and we were proud that we could deliver the bombs with a very high degree of accuracy. The F-100 had been built in the 1950s as our first fighter capable of supersonic speed in level flight, but in Vietnam it was a mud mover, *par excellence.*

Colonel Donald W. Kilgus

The Republic F-105 Thunderchief, the Thud? There wasn't anybody else in the Thud to keep you out of trouble. It was a single-seat airplane.

The canopy rail on the Thud is about 13 feet off the ground. That's where your elbow is. When you're sitting in that airplane taxiing out, you're the king of the world.

The one thing it did was, when you got down low and you

started going fast, it had a variable ratio feedback in the flight control system so that if you were going 1,000 knots and you pulled a quarter of an inch, you got a millimeter of deflection on the stabilizer. The faster you went, the steadier it felt.

Shooting the cannon you could use explosive, incendiary, armor-piercing, whatever. The shell goes out at 3,250 feet per second. When you fire that M61 cannon it just goes "hummm" and it cuts down everything in its path.

At one point in the 1967-68 period, somebody calculated that it was mathematically impossible for *any* Thud pilot to complete 100 combat missions over North Vietnam and survive. In fact, we lost more than half of the entire F-105 production run up around Hanoi. But don't forget that we delivered millions of pounds of bombload in the face of the heaviest air defenses the world has ever seen. We shot down a fair number of MiGs, too. The Thud was big. A big plane, a big engine, and it dished out ten times as much punishment as it received. It was a heck of a plane.

Captain Gary Wendell

There's a time for a light touch and a time for brute force. You've seen the boxing match where the welterweight is dancing about on his feet, testing and sparring, using style and deception and a little art. In the F-4 Phantom, it's like you're the heavyweight who defeats the other guy by rolling over him like a ton of bricks. You don't want to get into a fight that will be decided on

continued on page 64

continued from page 62

the basis of talent or style. You want to roll over top of the other guy like a railroad train and make sure he's been smashed before he has a chance to do anything. The Phantom was designed to engage from up to 30 miles. At that distance, the Phantom was supreme. So you wanted to hit the other guy from a distance and roll over him like an express train.

Sometimes, though, you'd get into a pointblank slugfest. This one day, we're up over some low haze along Thud Ridge and my flight lead cries out, "MiGs at seven o'clock!" We had zero warning. "I got 'em," my front-seater said. If you anticipated it right, you could pull the Phantom around in a pretty sharp turn, plug in burner, and come out of the turn with enough energy to have the bounce on the other guy. This time, our number three elected to set himself up to give us a shot. "He's on to me!" shouted Three. "He's a MiG-21, MiG-21! I'm gonna stretch him out for you, baby! . . ." Three allowed himself to become a perfect target for the MiG so that we could turn, plug in, finish the

turn, and suddenly have the whole sky ahead of us filled with this gigantic silvery expanse of enemy airplane.

Our gun jammed. So help me. Here's Wendell's chance for glory and our gun jammed. We'd finally put the M61A1 Gatling gun on the F-4E version of the Phantom and it generally worked pretty well but this time we had a misfire. It took the MiG a fairly [long time], maybe ten seconds, to realize that we had him nailed and he managed a break that got him out of there. . . .

A US Air Force colonel

The Northrop F-5A Freedom Fighter and F-5E Tiger were developed for exactly the kind of situation that unfolded in 'Nam— an armed struggle in the Third World where a friendly country wanted and needed its own fighter aircraft but did not necessarily need the "top of the line" fighter from our inventory. When I flew with the Vietnamese in the F-5, there was a wide diversity of experience among their maintenance people and pilots.

Some were very experienced and had been fighting the bad guys ever since the French were here. They had no tour of duty to finish, no home to go to, not like us. They simply fought on and on. Others were less experienced. The F-5 was ideal for either group. It was a "state of the art" supersonic fighter but it was designed for Third World operators with a range of abilities.

I was flying the F-5A Freedom Fighter over there. Once down near the Mekong Delta I found myself with a lot of small-arms fire whining around me, and slugs crunching into the thin metal skin of the aircraft, and I said to myself, "This is a real hot seat!" The F-5 maneuvers like a crazed mongoose and I just zigged and zagged through all that gunfire. The bad news is, the airplane doesn't sustain damage very well. It's a good fighter in which to *avoid* getting hit but not a good one in which to *take* hits, so those I *did* take were serious. How'd you like to have black oil spraying into your face from a hydraulics leak? I was damned lucky to limp home.

Previous page

Not long after arrival in the battle zone, Huns and other jet fighters began to acquire camouflage paint schemes, sometimes called T. O. 1-1-4 camouflage after the technical order which prescribed them. Newly attired in this war paint, F-100D Super Sabre 55-3595 of the Silver Knights sets forth from Saigon's Tan Son Nhut airbase in about June 1966 carrying a load of CBU-2 cluster bombs. Donald W. Kilgus

At one time the 20th Tactical Reconnaissance Squadron at Udorn, Thailand, had more planes than pilots, but still mounted a reconnaissance mission over North Vietnam every morning and afternoon. Known as the Green Pythons, the squadron took RF-101C Voodoos, like this one in August 1967, on the fastest missions ever flown by Americans in combat. Ray Carlson

El Viejo Cazador *(The Old Hunter),* alias *F-100D Super Sabre 56-3053 of the 510th Tactical Fighter Squadron, 3rd Tactical Fighter Wing—Jack Doub at the controls— lifts off from Bien Hoa in October 1969. Although in the midst of a shooting war, this is a training flight, the aircraft carries no ordnance under its wings.* Jack Doub

Another view of F-105F Wild Weasel pilot Don Kilgus looking around alertly for missiles, MiGs or anti-aircraft fire. Donald W. Kilgus

68

*Immediately after their return
from the Southeast Asia conflict,
Thuds of the 561st Tactical Fighter
Squadron work out over the
southwest American desert in
December 1972. Aircraft 63-4359
(MD tailcode) stationed at
McConnell AFB, Kansas, is
carrying a blue AGM-78A
Standard ARM training round.*
Donald W. Kilgus

70

Aboard the carrier USS Midway
*(CVA-41), F-4J Phantom 153872
(side number NF-116) of the
Chargers of VF-161 prepares to be
hurtled into the air by the ship's
steam catapult. Phantoms from*
Midway *shot down the first and
last MiGs to be destroyed during
the conflict.* Steven W. Daniels

*One of the most beautiful paint
schemes ever applied to a Phantom
belonged to the Death Angels of
VMFA-235 who, when not in the
war zone, basked in the idyllic
setting of MCAS Kaneohe Bay,
Hawaii. Unfortunately, the white
stars and red field on the radome
interfered with the operation of the
radar and was soon replaced.*
Joseph G. Handelman

F-4J Phantom 155749 (side number DB-12) of the Death Angels of VMFA-235 during a visit to MCAS Yuma, Arizona. Marine Corps Phantoms were among the first US aircraft to arrive in the Southeast Asia battle zone and among the last to leave. Robert F. Dorr

The Pacemakers of VF-21 provided fleet readiness training to every squadron that went to the Gulf of Tonkin to take the war to the North Vietnamese. Postwar view shows F-4J Phantom 155769 (side number NJ-145) of the Pacemakers during a visit to NAS Oceana, Virginia, on 15 October 1978. Robert F. Dorr

The F-4B version of the Phantom II made the first and last MiG kills of the war. Aircraft 152217, at Andrews AFB, Maryland, on 9 June 1977, was the very last F-4B model to fly. Markings on fuselage are standard for Hell's Angels of VMFA-321, but tail markings are an experiment which was not adopted when the squadron converted to F-4N. Robert F. Dorr

Two Northrop F-5A Freedom Fighters (63-8428 and 65-10580) of the South Vietnamese Air Force (VNAF) cruising above a typical Southeast Asia build-up of clouds on a combat mission in November 1970. F-5A and its successor, F-5E, were the most advanced jet fighters employed by the VNAF. Cort Durocher

Dissimilar air combat maneuver training was the key to success against Hanoi's MiGs in the 1972 fighting and has become a keystone of both Navy and Air Force operations ever since, with the F-5 serving until recently as an aggressor to imitate the role of the enemy fighter. F-5E Tiger II 74-1575 of the Air Force's 3rd Tactical Fighter Wing is seen at Clark AB, Philippines, in January 1981. F-5E Tiger II 159882 of the US Navy's Fighter Weapons School (Top Gun) is at NAS Miramar, California, in 1977. Chris Pocock and M. P. Curphey

Who *are* those guys?

Captain Charles Blandenton

I'm a navigator on a B-52 so I'm accustomed to hearing people say that the aerial campaigns in Vietnam were decided by the B-52 Stratofortress or the F-4 Phantom. That's bunk. I don't want to play down my own guys or the fighters either, but not a single combat mission in Southeast Asia would have been worth a hoot without the contribution of the combat support people who flew every aircraft type from the KC-135 tanker to the HH-43 helicopter.

If you were aboard a big bomber or were blazing through the sky as a hot-rock fighter jock, you knew at least that you were the stuff they put on recruiting posters. Very often, the public never heard anything at all about the "other guys"—the overwhelming majority of aviation people and air crews who flew the lesser-known aircraft and carried out their jobs with a minimum of fanfare.

My hat is off to the people who did the very difficult, grueling, often very hazardous reconnaissance, refueling and rescue missions.

Designer Edward H. Heinemann

Having made many flights in the Douglas A-3 Skywarrior from both land and aircraft carriers, I must say it was always a thrill especially to feel that "kick in the pants" when being catapulted from a carrier. I was rather proud

continued on page 88

The Whale, or A-3 (formerly A3D) Skywarrior, flew bomber, tanker, electronic and trainer missions in the Vietnam conflict and survived to fly another day. In a sun-drenched postwar setting, TA-3B Skywarrior 144356 (side number GD-21) of squadron VAQ-33 basks at NAS Oceana, Virginia, on 15 October 1978. This aircraft carries a long "probe" for in-flight refueling and has had passenger accommodations, including windows, added to its former bomb bay. Robert F. Dorr

Bien Hoa airbase, about 40 miles from Saigon, was used from the beginning of the conflict until its end. Not immediately visible is the Kaman HH-43F Huskie rescue helicopter hovering in front of the control tower. The HH-43F was intended for local airbase rescue but on occasion actually saved downed pilots inside North Vietnam. Cort Durocher

continued from page 84

of this bird perhaps mainly because we did the impossible and built a machine for 68,000 pounds when the Navy's own spec said 100,000 pounds and others said it couldn't be done for less than 150,000.

[When we designed the A3D-1 Skywarrior in 1950], the principal requirements were to carry a 10,000 pound device five feet by five feet by sixteen feet in length, suspected to be an atomic bomb, a distance of 2,000 mile radius. The details of the bomb were so secret that for a long time we didn't even have a drawing. We knew a certain element had to be inserted in flight through a door from the cockpit, which further complicated the problem.

The competition was between North American, Curtiss Wright, Douglas, and possibly others. North American turned in no bid because they said it could not be done for 100,000 pounds. [We built the first A3D-1 Skywarrior] for 68,000 pounds but it took a great deal of discipline and tough engineering management to do so, and I must admit that to hold the 68,000 pounds, whenever the Navy added a pound of weight we took out a pound of fuel.

continued on page 90

Almost unknown even to serious researchers of the war is the fact that the US Air Force operated its own squadron of Huey helicopters in Vietnam. An unusual mixture of early-morning rain and haze gives a shimmering quality to the rotors of UH-1F Huey of the Green Hornets 20th Special Operations Squadron at Ban My Thuet in 1968. Joe Viviano

continued from page 88
A total of 282 airplanes were built in some six or seven versions with the first contract calling for two flight tests and one static test or the equivalent of three aircraft with a total price of $14,650,000. By the time the first airplanes were built, a smaller [atomic] bomb became available and by the time the airplanes were deployed in the fleet a still smaller model was available. Had there not been so much bomb secrecy a smaller airplane could have been built compatible with the production bombs that would have resulted in a gross weight of 50,000 pounds or less and, of course, corresponding dollar savings.

Rear Admiral William B. Dorsey

The A-3 was designed as a nuclear bomb carrier, all right, and in Southeast Asia we used it for everything but. As a matter of fact, the A-3 had only a very brief life as a *conventional* bomber, for we felt that was just too much airplane to be lobbing 500 pounders at a bunch of Viet Cong scurrying around in the jungle. I remember we sent one guy up on a mission from Connie [the carrier USS *Constellation* (CVA-64)] and he drove his Whale out to find what they called a "suspected Viet Cong position." He took several small-arms hits which seriously wounded his co-pilot and he *never saw* any of the Viet Cong who were hit by his bombs.

Yes, we called it the Whale. It was an awkward aircraft to land on a carrier and looked very funny coming in, so we called *that* the Whale Dance. We had the KA-3, EA-3 and TA-3 versions of the

90

airplane for the tanker, electronics and trainer missions. The Whale was a tough and ugly brute of an airplane, and it could be hot as blazes inside the flight cabin on a blistering day, but it was thoroughly reliable. Only six were lost in combat in the entire war, and that included one which simply vanished in the South China Sea. Charlie just wasn't going to shoot down one of those A-3s on us if we could possibly prevent it.

Colonel John Bull Stirling

The reconnaissance guys in the RF-101C Voodoo probably contributed more to the combat effort than anyone else, including the much more publicized MiG killers.

The McDonnell RF-101C Voodoo was still perhaps the highest-performing warplane in the world two decades after being sketched out on paper, a decade after entering service. The product of a company that was unknown when it was conceived, the Voodoo was the butt of an airmen's bar-room ballad which called it a widowmaker and was more difficult to fly than any fighter ever to attain squadron service with the

continued on page 92

Returning from a combat mission over North Vietnam, RF-101C Voodoo at Udorn—a reconnaissance aircraft based upon a "century series" fighter—uses its air-refueling probe to give the finger to on-watchers as the skipper of the 20th Tactical Fighter Squadron completes his 100th mission "up north." John Bull Stirling

continued from page 90

US Air Force. It was known for pitching up and it had a nosewheel that wouldn't retract, sometimes, but in addition to being a powerful fighter the camera package in the nose made it an exceedingly effective flying photo platform. Those cameras and the Voodoo's instruments regularly went on the blink in Udorn's terrible heat, while its tires disagreed mightily with the Thai airfield's concave runway and steel-plank revetments. After years in silver and gray, the Voodoo was painted finally in the T. O. 1-1-4 camouflage of the Vietnam war. And a warplane it *was,* propelled by afterburning Pratt & Whitney J57-P-13 turbojets; the Voodoo not only *exuded* speed and power, it *had* both.

Colonel Harry F. Wilson, Jr., KC-135 navigator

The Boeing KC-135 Stratotanker, or the "One Thirty Five" as we usually called it, was in the Southeast Asia conflict beginning with the Young Tiger task force which deployed in 1964. The tankers remained under the

continued on page 94

Not as glamorous as shooting down MiGs, the job of the "other guys" in Marine Corps aviation, as Marines themselves quickly point out, is to support the rifleman on the ground. In Southeast Asia, the Huey Cobra gunship introduced the notion of a helicopter designed from the outset for the air-to-ground combat mission. In later years, the Cobra has been refined and developed. AH-1J Cobra 157772 of squadron HML-367 practices at Camp Fuji, Japan, in 1976. Robert F. Dorr

92

continued from page 92

jurisdiction of SAC, the Strategic Air Command, throughout the war. Unlike others, [they] maintained "hard" aircraft crews with the same people flying together all the time as pilot, co-pilot, navigator and boom operator.

Ours were called combat support missions but at times we made the difference between success and failure in battle: More than once a quick refuel or even a hasty "tow" by a KC-135 saved a Thud or Phantom that had been crippled by enemy gunfire over North Vietnam. The tanker crews always received high praise from the guys we served, and the KC-135—which had been designed from the outset for the tanker mission—served brilliantly.

Colonel M. P. Curphey

When we first started into Vietnam in the Kennedy years, the Air Force's Air Commandos took a few B-26 Invaders over and flew in combat with them whilst maintaining the fiction that it was a Vietnamese war. The aircraft, originally called the A-26, had been successful in World War II and Korea but by the time we got to 'Nam they had too many hours

continued on page 96

The RF-101C Voodoo was the first US aircraft in squadron service to arrive in South Vietnam, arriving at Saigon's Tan Son Nhut Airport in 1961. At one point when the airbase ran out of jet engine fuel, KB-50 Superfortress tankers were brought in to refuel the Voodoos on the ground. This extraordinary event, not previously depicted in any publication, is shown in this unusual view of the war's earliest days. A. Robert Gould

94

continued from page 94
on the frames and there was a major structural problem with the wing pylons that were being used to carry 750 lb bombs. After a series of crashes which were attributed to the *wings falling off,* the B-26 was withdrawn from the combat zone.

Later on, improved B-26s were moved into Nakhon Phanom, Thailand, where they used the callsign NIMROD and flew day and

night missions against the North Vietnamese infiltration route, the Ho Chi Minh Trail. These newer B-26s had been extensively rebuilt and did not have the structural flaws that were discovered earlier in the war. The Nimrods were not quite fish or fowl, and no reporters were allowed at Nakhon Phanom anyway, so they never made the newspapers—but they did a bang-up job of choking off enemy supply convoys.

In 1972 as combat operations were stepped up over North Vietnam, Seymour Johnson AFB, South Carolina-based F-4E Phantoms were deployed to Southeast Asia in a hurry. One of these Seymour birds is being refueled on a combat mission by Boeing KC-135A Stratotanker 56-3631. Randy Thomas

The archetypical RF-101C Voodoo pilot of the Vietnam War era. Captain A. Robert Gould was in Vietnam in 1961 with the Voodoo, one of the first Americans to arrive in the battle zone. In this view taken a few years later, Lieutenant Colonel Gould is seen with his Voodoo at a European base where his aircraft has been zapped by the Bumble Bee of the German squadron AkG 51. A. Robert Gould

B-26K Invader 44-34766 Mary Jo, veteran of the Nimrods 609th Special Operations Squadron at Nakhon Phanom, retains its Vietnam-era markings after being retired to an outdoor display at Castle AFB, California, on 26 December 1982. B-26 Invaders served in World War II, Korea and Vietnam. Donald S. McGarry

The reconnaissance version of the Crusader served in Southeast Asia from the beginning of the war to the end, and later became the final version of the F-8 to fly. RF-8G Crusader 146882 (side number NA-603) of Reserve squadron VFP-306 gets a tractor haul during maintenance work at Andrews AFB, Maryland, on 17 March 1979. Robert F. Dorr

Previous page

The Air Force's twin-engine version of the ubiquitous Huey, perhaps the best-known aircraft of the Vietnam War, continues to soldier on. UH-1N Huey 69-6619, belonging to Detachment 6 of the 40th Aerospace Rescue and Recovery Service, awaits work before its next flight at Holloman AFB, New Mexico, on 26 December 1980. M. J. Kasiuba

Probably the most obscure US Air Force aircraft from the Southeast Asia war was the Helio U-10 Courier, a short takeoff/landing (STOL) plane capable of operating from unprepared airfields. Even more obscure, and considered by me to be one of the most puzzling photos of the war, is this view of U-10 5907A in bogus South Vietnamese markings, apparently at Ban My Thuet in 1964. Purpose of the message beneath the Courier's wings is not known. Donald W. Kilgus

The MiG killers

Manfred Von Richthofen

The fighter pilots have to rove in an area allotted to them in any way they like, and when they spot an enemy they attack and shoot him down. Anything else is rubbish.

Major Philip P. Combies

We were flying at 16,000 feet mean sea level and 540 knots true air speed. Shortly after completing the turn to the northwest we spotted a flight of four MiG-21s in loose formation, two o'clock low at approximately six to eight miles. Approximately one to two miles behind were two more MiG-21s, making a total of six observed. Due to their position "ahead of the beam," I wonder now if they were being vectored against us or possibly against [other American pilots] who were initiating their egress from the area.

As the MiGs crossed in front of [Captain J. B.] Stone, he started in on them, breaking left and down. This caused the flight to slide to the right and I wound up high and right from the remainder of flight. I went "burner" and held

continued on page 106

In 1972, when combat operations resumed over North Vietnam, the 4th Tactical Fighter Wing from Seymour Johnson AFB, North Carolina, was rushed over so fast that its aircraft arrived in plain-Jane markings. F-4E Phantom 66-327 with the wing's SJ tailcode is heading toward Hanoi carrying a pair of Paveway "smart" bombs.
Randy Thomas

continued from page 105

minimum "burner" throughout the initial engagement. The MiGs broke left and our flight commenced the engagement. My pilot secured, by boresight, a full system lock-on on one of the MiGs. I had selected radar and interlocks out, as prebriefed for an Air Combat Tactics environment. I had no difficulty in tracking the MiG. I don't think I pulled over four Gs at any time during the whole battle. Using the Navy tactic of disregarding the steering dot, I pulled lead on the MiG using the reticle. When I felt I was where I wanted to be, I pulled the trigger, released, pulled again, and held. I did not observe the first Sparrow at all. However, I saw the second from launch to impact. We were approximately one mile behind the MiG, in a left turn, at approximately 12,000 feet at the time of launch. The second Sparrow impacted in the tailpipe area followed by a large orange ball of fire and a chute sighting.

Colonel Andrew Baird

MiG! The first warning is usually a call from DISCO, the radar picket plane out over the Gulf, or from RED CROWN, the Navy ship which prowls the coast and keeps its radars locked on Hanoi's air force. Sometimes, though, all of our sophisticated detection breaks down. Sometimes you hear the word "MiG!" from your own Flight Leader, telling you that without any warning you've just been sandbagged by North Vietnamese fighters. They work hard to set up an ambush. Sometimes they succeed. That's when your flight leader has that twangy extra tone of urgency in his voice and you sense that you're in real trouble. "MiGs! Bandits at seven o'clock, high! More at nine o'clock! There's MiGs all over us, guys!"

So the fight comes down, as it always must, to a contest between man and man. Our F-4 Phantom is better in combat at missile range and has a better radar. Their MiG-17 is more maneuverable and has a very potent cannon. Our jet is better in some situations, theirs in others. But it's always the man, in the end. In the 1965-68 campaigns our pilots were older and had more experience but had not been aggressively trained. In the 1972 campaign, the American fighter pilot was younger but was also the product of some well-thought, rigorous air combat training. In both situations our pilots were better than theirs—though it's surprising how good theirs were—but we prevailed by only a narrow margin.

You fight with radar-guided missiles. You fight with heat-seekers like the Sidewinder. You fight with guns. There can be some very traumatic twisting and turning up there in the high cold arena of the sky and, in the final analysis, what you fight with is your wits. If you're lucky, of course, you can swat down that MiG with a Sparrow missile from fifteen miles away, but it doesn't usually happen that way. In fact, you don't usually have the initiative. The war over North Vietnam may have been the first where all the advantages went to the defender rather than the attacker. Anyway, it usually becomes a close-quarters brawl. While we had pretty good airplanes, most of them, we scored more air-to-air shootdowns because we had *very* good pilots.

Lieutenant Commander Thomas W. Swenson

It has been widely reported that carrier aviation is so dangerous, naval aviators are more apprehensive about landing on a ship's deck than about going into combat. It's true, or at least it *was* true, but I think the North Vietnamese managed to change that. In 1968, we heard that they had 1,900 anti-aircraft gun batteries, 36 SAM sites, and 200 MiGs. This gave them a couple of thousand different ways to try to kill us.

During the 1967-68 fighting over North Vietnam, when we were losing a lot of people and being confronted by MiGs almost daily, we had high spirits and a real sense of sharing the burden. We also had some of the most brightly painted airplanes in the US Navy, too, because we were allowed to apply trim, squadron markings, and MiG kills to our Phantoms and Crusaders. In spite of the frustrations of the war—which meant, particularly, losing guys from our squadron, since this was far more personal than anything happening back home—we had the belief that we were doing a good job and that we could beat the North Vietnamese if given half the chance. I don't think anyone in the entire Vietnam war contributed more than the incredible maintenance guys who worked on the aircraft at night, in

continued on page 108

City of Fairborn *F-4D Phantom 66-7554 belongs to the Air Force Reserve's 89th Tactical Fighter Squadron at Dayton, Ohio. On 6 November 1967, Captain Darrell D. Simmonds and 1st Lt. George H. McKinney, Jr., shot down two MiG-17s aboard this Phantom, using a centerline 20 mm cannon. David W. Menard*

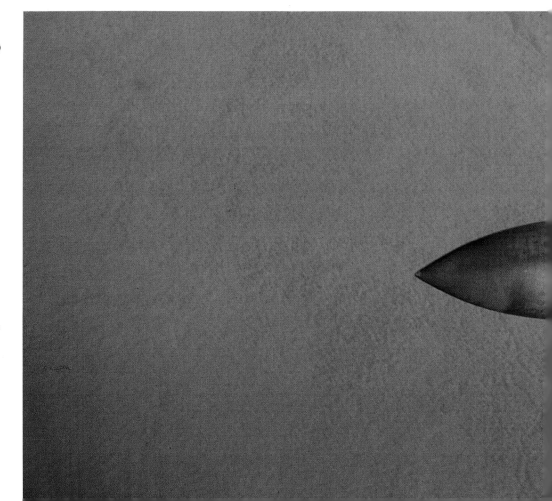

continued from page 106

the carrier's hangar bays, in the glare of bright artificial lights, performing miracles with their wrenches. We may have flown the jets and fought the MiGs but it took thousands of guys to make it happen.

Colonel D. J. Kiely

I joined the Marine Corps to fly the F-8 Crusader because it was the hottest thing in the air, it was a flying blowtorch. The *real* fighter pilots are single-seat, single-engine guys and the Crusader, with that afterburning J57 was a fighter pilot's fighter—fast, nimble, maneuverable and heavily armed. It was conceived to fight the bad guys up in the air, but later in the war we had them with hard points on the wings to carry bombs and the F-8 proved very successful against ground targets. I went in under clouds during the Battle of

continued on page 110

Few fighters, whether they shot down MiGs or not, inspired the imagination as much as the Vought F-8 Crusader; pilots regarded it as the last single-seat, single-engine, cannon-armed air combat machine. F-8J Crusader (ex-F-8E) 149204 (side number NP-206) of squadron VF-24 shows off its colors and shape at NAS Miramar, California, on 1 November 1975. Don Logan

Colonel Robin Olds' famous Wolfpack in action. At the height of fighting against Hanoi's MiG force in early 1967, an F-4C Phantom of Olds' 8th Tactical Fighter Wing from Ubon, Thailand, joins up over greenery, en route home from North Vietnam. Truman Spangrud

108

continued from page 108
Hue at the time of the Tet Offensive, found myself in a head-on duel with a machine-gunner in a tower over the city, and managed to wax him with some precision low-level strafing. If the F-8 Crusader was nothing else, it was *reliable* and a lot of Ho Chi Minh's

followers didn't make it through the war simply because that airplane did exactly what it was supposed to do.

The Marines didn't shoot down any MiGs with the Crusader, but Navy Crusader pilots managed to reduce Ho Chi Minh's MiG-17 and MiG-21 inventory by some

twenty airplanes. Most of those MiG kills were scored with Sidewinder missiles, but the Crusader could make *very* effective use of its 20 mm cannons. We used to say, "When you're out of F-8s, you're out of fighters."

Returning from the final combat mission. Caroline, *better known as F-4D Phantom 66-7767 (FG) of the 433rd Tactical Fighter Squadron, 8th Tactical Fighter Wing, Ubon, Thailand, is effusively trailing colored smoke as the two-man crew completes its all-important 100th combat mission over North Vietnam. Pilot Captain Steve Mosier steps out of Caroline to accept the ritual champagne. Steve Mosier*

Sky. Night. War. Using the formation strip lights which were added only about midway into the war, an F-4E Phantom of the 421st Tactical Fighter Squadron, part of the 432nd Tactical Fighter Wing, bores through Vietnamese skies in 1972. Spider Scharett

In a unique and little-known paint scheme, F-8K Crusader 146918 (side number MG-6) of the Hell's Angels of VMF-321 poses at Andrews AFB, Maryland, on 27 April 1972. Twenty North Vietnamese MiGs were shot down by Crusaders, including two shot down partly or fully with 20 mm cannon fire. Stephen H. Miller

Previous page

Only one MiG was ever shot down by the ground-attack Douglas A-4 Skyhawk. But the Scooter did a superb job of hitting the enemy on the ground and two-seat versions of the Skyhawk served as Forward Air Controllers, or FACs. Others trained the men who went to war: TA-4J Skyhawk 153465 (side number 3F-201) is in flight over the United States in July 1973. Bob Thomas

Republic F-105D Thunderchief, nicknamed the Thud. It carried bombs to Hanoi, fired rockets into enemy SAM sites, and shot down a couple of dozen MiGs. Thunderchief 62-4361 belongs to the 419th Tactical Fighter Wing, an Air Force Reserve unit at Hill AFB, Utah, and is flying over the American southwest on 28 September 1983. Lindsay T. Peacock

Survivors

Captain Alexander Trujillo

They say the F-4 Phantom is no longer a front-line fighter in today's world. That's bull. I remember when we were doing two-versus-two against F-15s out of Bitburg. They're supposed to have a better radar, but I spotted them before they spotted us. I painted the Eagles and passed it to my pilot in the front seat of our F-4D. "Fight's on," he said and I confirmed, "Fight's on, camera's on."

We twisted and turned with the highly maneuverable F-15 and our F-4, which requires some knowledge and nursing, stayed with them most of the time. At Sidewinder range, it was about an equal fight. Once into gun range, of course, our Phantom was just about useless. It always had been without a gun. I can tell you, though, that even with the world famous Eagle there were times we could outmaneuver him and get on his six and we could kill him *if only we had a gun!*

Lieutenant Commander Robert V. Barr

So I say, "Hey, that airplane looks suspiciously like the same one I was flying off the *Kitty Hawk* on Yankee Station fifteen years ago." This is in 1980. So the skipper of our Naval Air Reserve squadron says, "You're right. And it wasn't even new *then.*" I'm not sure if anybody realizes how we manufacture aircraft for their longevity.

Look at some of the best-known fighters of World War II. Some of them were designed, built, tested, put into service, flown in combat, and retired from duty *all in the span of four to eight years.* From the Vietnam era up to the present it's been a very different story. The A-4 Skyhawk is still flying and it's been around since the early 1950s. The F-8 Crusader served for more than three decades before we finally retired her only in 1987. The F-4 Phantom made its first flight in 1958 and, while the Navy doesn't use the F-4 aboard carriers anymore, it's still a front-line fighter in a lot of places. And the all-time "World Book of Records" winner has to be the B-52 Stratofortress, which was already very old when it started flying missions in 'Nam. The B-52 was designed in the 1940s and is now the longest-serving warplane in the history of aviation.

Of course, most of the warplanes from the Vietnam period have now gone to the boneyard or found themselves in museums. Some have become "gate guards"—the term for a retired

continued on page 120

At the US Naval Academy in Annapolis, Maryland, F-4A Phantom 148275 (side number AC-200) appears on display in the markings of the Swordsmen of the squadron VF-32. This Phantom was an early developmental craft and helped produce the F-4B and F-4J Phantoms which flew from carrier decks in the Gulf of Tonkin. Joseph G. Handelman

continued from page 118
warrior placed on outdoor display where the next generation will be able to see it. It's important that we preserve these machines from our history. I hope to be able to look at and touch Skyhawks, Crusaders and Phantoms in the next century, long after no one is flying them anyplace.

Master Sergeant David W. Menard

In past wars, we've always been very quick to dispose of combat aircraft once the fighting was finished. In late 1945, thousands of P-38s, P-47s and P-51s were junked, scrapped, or pushed into the sea leaving very few examples to be preserved and looked at by future generations. After the Korean armistice in 1953, almost no attempt was made to salvage F9Fs, F-86s, or other aircraft that had fought in the conflict. We are doing a little better today—many bases have museums—and, of course, many of the aircraft from the Vietnam war are still flying operationally. So there will be *real* examples of our real combat aircraft around for some years to come.

Senior Master Sergeant Tom Brewer

We've always turned in mixed results when it comes to honoring our history and making sure that we who live in the present do not forget the important events of the past. As incredible as it must seem, the Air Force did not keep a record of the serial numbers of aircraft which shot down MiGs in Southeast Asia. The Air Force does not presently have an official

listing, and we are trying to put one together.

Does anyone out there remember which F-4C was being flown by Martin and Krieps when they shot down a MiG-21 on July 14, 1966? Does anyone know which F-4D Howerton and Voight were using when they got a MiG-17 on February 14, 1968? How about the F-105D Thunderchiefs used by Tolman, Eskew, Gast and Kuster to shoot down MiG-17s? Some of these American aircraft are still in existence but their status as MiG killers has never been documented and they've never been painted accordingly. Anyone who can help the Air Force Museum fill these "gaps" in our history is requested to contact the Friends of the Air Force Museum, P.O. Box 1903, Wright-Patterson AFB, Ohio 45433.

The Museum has done a remarkable job of restoring a few examples of these mechanical veterans of the Vietnam conflict, including an F-4C Phantom flown by Robin Olds for two of his four MiG kills. We need to continue to try to preserve some of the conglomerations of steel and plexiglass and plastic that fought our war for us, as a way of paying tribute to the *men* who fought the war.

Brigadier General Robin Olds, seeing his MiG-killer Phantom at the Air Force Museum

Old 829 looks as though she were a 45-year-old spinster all made up, primped and permed, trying to look as though she were still a teenager about to go to the high school prom. I can't describe my feelings when I sat in that

cockpit. It was like a time warp. All my senses responded to the familiarity of those dials and switches and I was filled with the emotions and mental tensions felt so often in that cockpit. It wasn't a "like yesterday" sensation. It was a "NOW—HERE—GOING ON."

That machine to me was a love affair. Load her with bombs and missiles, hang tanks and an ECM pod, strip her of her makeup—and you've got a tiger that will hurtle you through the air with a ferocity matching that of her crew. Unload your ordnance and she's a thing of fury, twisting, turning in a three-dimensional arena like a demon in hell—then quietly taking you home to the tanker and your runway through the towering cumulus of Thailand, beauty herself in God's beauty.

The mighty HH-53C Super Jolly Green Giant helicopters which flew rescue missions deep into North Vietnam remain in service today and continue to rescue downed airmen. HH-53C 69-5784 of the 67th Aerospace Rescue and Recovery Squadron, seen at RAF Woodbridge, England, on 6 September 1985, is one veteran of combat in Southeast Asia. Cylindrical refueling probe gives the helicopter a distinctive look.
Robert F. Dorr

A-7D Corsair 69-6192—painted to represent aircraft 70-970 of the 354th Tactical Fighter Wing, Korat AB, Thailand—at the Air Force Museum in 1987. Flying airplane 70-970, Major Arnie Clarke carried out a ten-hour Sandy mission, or combat rescue mission, under heavy fire in November 1972, repeatedly cycling off the tanker to protect downed air crewmen who eventually were rescued. Clarke was awarded the Air Force Cross. David W. Menard

Although far from new when it began supporting Vietnam combat operations in 1964, the Boeing KC-135 Stratotanker remains the principal air-refueling tanker of the US Air Force today. Aircraft 59-1521, an early Stratotanker retrofitted with CFM56 engines and now known as a KC-135R, paused for a visit at Andrews AFB, Maryland, on 7 May 1988. Robert F. Dorr

Previous page
Immaculately restored in the markings it wore when Colonel Robin Olds scored two of his four MiG kills in it, F-4C Phantom 64-829 basks in the sun at the Air Force Museum, Dayton, Ohio, in 1988. Flying with the Wolfpack, or 8th Tactical Fighter Wing, commanded by Olds, this Phantom became one of the best-known of the war. David W. Menard

In 1988, the Strategic Air Command announced that four wings of B-52 Stratofortress bombers would take on the conventional bombing mission, to complement the nuclear bombing role performed by other Stratofortress units. It must have given some SAC crews a sense of deja vu. *The B-52 was designed to carry atomic bombs, but from 1965 to 1973, it dropped conventional ordnance in Southeast Asia—with significant effect on the bad guys.* Jim Benson

126

MiG killer Phantom, alias F-4D
66-7554, seen in close-up during its
30 April 1988 visit to Andrews
AFB, Maryland. Robert F. Dorr